PERFECTLY IMPERFECT

MASTERING THE ART OF AWKWARD AWESOMENESS

GARIMA VAISHYA

To the brave souls, the imperfectly awesome humans, who realized that being awkward is just another way to be awesome, to those who learned to love their chaos.

Contents

Contents

Introduction

Welcome to the ultimate self-help guide that doesn't take itself too seriously. Life's a mess, and so are we, but that doesn't mean we can't have a good laugh while figuring things out. This book is for anyone who's ever tripped over their own shoelaces while trying to "run their life." Spoiler alert: we all have.

Through funny anecdotes, brutally honest advice, and a sprinkle of motivation, we'll tackle everything from dealing with self-doubt to discovering your true potential—without the boring lectures or the "you can do it!" posters. So grab a cup of coffee, tea, or whatever keeps you going, and let's dive in!

CHAPTER ONE

THE ART OF MESSING UP (AND OWNING IT)

The Time I Majorly Messed Up (And Didn't Die)

Let's start with a confession: I have messed up. A lot. Like, a lot a lot.

There was this one time I confidently walked into class, sat down, took out my books—only to realize I was in the wrong classroom. Worse? The actual students and teacher were staring at me like I had just crash-landed from another planet.

My brain? FULL PANIC MODE.

"Do I slowly back away? Pretend I belong here? Crawl under the desk and start a new life as a floor mat?"

In the end, I awkwardly mumbled "Oops, wrong class" and made a quick escape. And guess what? No one cared. Nobody pointed and laughed, no one made a meme out of me (that I know of), and the world kept spinning.

That's when I learned something: messing up isn't the problem—how we handle it is.

Why Messing Up Feels Like the End of the World (But Isn't)

We all hate making mistakes. It feels embarrassing, awkward, and like the entire universe is zooming in on our failure. But here's the truth: nobody is keeping track of your mistakes like you are.

People forget things faster than you think. (Remember when someone else messed up? No? Exactly.)

Everyone is too busy worrying about their own mistakes.

The biggest failures usually make the best stories later.

The problem isn't messing up—it's that we let our mistakes define us.

Aha Moment: Everyone Messes Up (Even the Coolest People You Know)

Think of someone you admire—maybe a celebrity, a teacher, or even your super-confident friend. Guess what? They've all made mistakes. Probably huge ones. They just learned to laugh, learn, and move on.

Take any successful person—they didn't get there by being perfect. They got there by failing, fixing, and trying again.

How to Mess Up Like a Pro (And Survive It)

✓ Step 1: Own It – The fastest way to move on? Admit it. Don't pretend it didn't happen, don't blame your cat, and don't try to Jedi mind-trick people into forgetting. Just own it. ("Yep, I totally just walked into a glass door. You're welcome for the entertainment.")

✓ Step 2: Laugh About It – Embarrassment shrinks when you turn it into a joke. The moment you make fun of yourself, you take away its power.

✓ Step 3: Learn and Move On – Every mistake teaches you something. Forgot your lines in a presentation? Now you know to practice more. Bombed a test? Time to change your study strategy. Messing up is only bad if you don't learn from it.

✓ Step 4: Remember—No One Cares as Much as You Think – Seriously. People are way too occupied with their own lives to spend time analyzing your blunders. (Unless you become an internet meme. Then... good luck.)

Final Thoughts (AKA Why This Chapter Matters)

Messing up isn't a sign of failure—it's a sign that you're trying. If you're not making mistakes, you're probably not pushing yourself enough.

So go ahead, mess up. Be awkward. Fall on your face (figuratively, preferably). Just make sure to laugh, learn, and get back up. Because the truth is, the people who succeed in life aren't the ones who never mess up—they're the ones who don't let it stop them.

And if you ever find yourself walking into the wrong class, just own it. Maybe even pretend you're a guest lecturer. Who knows? You might just pull it off.

CHAPTER TWO

Your Comfort Zone is a Lie

That Time I Almost Chickened Out

Picture this: It's Annual Day at school, and somehow, against my better judgment, I signed up for a dance performance. Now, let me clarify—I am not the "confidently twirl on stage" kind of person. More like the "hide in the back and hope no one notices me" type.

But there I was, standing behind the stage, heart hammering, regretting every life decision that led me to this moment. My brain went into full sabotage mode:

"What if I mess up?"

"What if I trip and become a viral fail video?"

"What if I completely forget the steps and just start doing jumping jacks?"

For a split second, I considered running. I mean, who really needs another dancer in a group performance anyway?

But then, the music started.

And before I could overthink myself into a coma, my body just... moved. One step. Then another. And just like that, I was dancing.

By the time it was over, something weird happened—I felt proud. Not because I was perfect (I definitely wasn't), but because I did it. I stepped out of my comfort zone, and instead of disaster, I found something better—confidence.

Your Comfort Zone is a Sneaky Little Liar

You know that cozy, safe feeling you get when you're in your routine, doing things you're good at, avoiding all risks? That's your comfort zone. And it feels nice—like a warm blanket on a cold day.

But here's the problem: nothing exciting ever happens there.

✓ You don't grow in your comfort zone.

✓ You don't discover new talents.

✓ You don't become the best version of yourself.

Instead, you just sit there, watching other people take chances, succeed, fail, learn, and grow—while you stay the same.

The "What If" Monster

Most of us don't stay in our comfort zones because we're lazy. We stay because of fear.

What if I fail?

What if people judge me?

What if I look stupid?

But here's a question: What if you don't?

What if you're actually good at it?

What if this one step leads to something amazing?

What if you're missing out on something that could change your life?

Your comfort zone tells you that staying safe is the best option. But growth, success, and the best moments of your life? They're waiting outside of it.

How to Escape the Comfort Zone (Without Having a Meltdown)

✓ Start Small – You don't have to go skydiving tomorrow. Just do one thing that feels slightly uncomfortable—answer a question in class, talk to someone new, try a new hobby.

✓ Say "Yes" Before You're Ready – Most of us wait until we

feel "prepared." Guess what? That day never comes. Just say yes, and figure it out as you go.

✓ Reframe Fear as Excitement – Your brain reacts to fear and excitement the same way. Instead of thinking "I'm terrified," tell yourself, "I'm excited to try this." It actually works.

✓ Fail on Purpose – Yep, you heard me. Mess up. Make mistakes. Show your brain that failure isn't the end of the world—it's just a stepping stone to getting better.

Final Thoughts (AKA Why You Need to Read This Again)

If you never step out of your comfort zone, you'll never know how much you're capable of. And trust me—you're capable of way more than you think.

So take the risk. Raise your hand. Join that competition. Try that new skill. The worst thing that can happen? You mess up and laugh about it later.

The best thing? You realize that your comfort zone was never protecting you—it was just holding you back.

CHAPTER THREE

The Comparison Trap (Hint: Everyone's Wingin' It)

That Time I Thought I Was the Only One Who Didn't Have It Together

There was a phase in my life (okay, maybe still ongoing) when I was convinced that everyone except me had their life figured out.

I'd scroll through social media, watching people ace exams, travel to cool places, and somehow always look perfect while doing it. Meanwhile, I was sitting in my pajamas, staring at my unfinished homework, wondering why my life didn't look as exciting.

I started thinking: Maybe I'm just not as smart. Not as talented. Not as put-together as everyone else.

And then one day, during a class test, I looked around and saw something interesting.

That girl who always seemed confident? Chewing her pen nervously.

That guy who always aced math? Whispering to his friend, "Bro, what's the answer to question 5?"

Even the teacher? Checking their notes because they didn't remember something.

That's when it hit me: Nobody actually knows what they're doing all the time. They're just good at pretending.

Why We Compare (And Why It's Dumb)

Comparison is something we all do, even without realizing it. And in today's world, it's worse than ever because of one thing—social media.

Here's the problem: we compare our behind-the-scenes with other people's highlight reels.

You see someone's perfect selfie, but not the 53 photos they took before choosing the best one.

You see someone winning awards, but not the hours they spent struggling to get there.

You see someone's confident speech, but not the nervous breakdown they had the night before.

We assume other people are effortlessly succeeding while we're the only ones struggling. But everyone is struggling—they just don't post it.

Aha Moment: The "Everyone is Faking It" Rule

You know how sometimes you have no idea what you're doing, but you pretend you do? Yeah, that's everyone.

That confident person? They're second-guessing themselves too.

That smart student? They've failed tests before.

That "perfect" influencer? They probably have bad hair days and embarrassing moments too.

Realizing this doesn't mean you stop improving. It just means you stop feeling less than because someone else seems ahead.

How to Escape the Comparison Trap (Without Deleting the Internet)

✓ Step 1: Focus on Your Own Progress – Instead of asking, "Why am I not as good as them?" ask, "Am I better than I was yesterday?" Small progress is still progress.

✓ Step 2: Take Social Media Breaks – If scrolling makes you

feel bad about yourself, stop scrolling. Remember, people only post the best 5% of their life—not the boring or messy 95%.

✓ Step 3: Turn Jealousy into Inspiration – Instead of thinking,"Ugh, they're so lucky," think, "If they can do it, I can too." Success isn't magic—it's effort.

✓ Step 4: Realize You're on Your Own Timeline – Just because someone else is ahead doesn't mean you're behind. Life isn't a race—it's a journey, and everyone moves at their own pace.

Final Thoughts (AKA Why This Chapter Matters)

Comparison steals joy. It makes you feel like you're never enough, even when you are.

So next time you catch yourself thinking someone else has a perfect life, remember: They're just wingin' it too. Instead of comparing, focus on your story, your progress, and your wins—big or small.

Because the truth? You're doing way better than you think.

CHAPTER FOUR

FEAR IS A DRAMA QUEEN (DON'T LET IT WIN)

The Time I Almost Let Fear Ruin Everything

Let's talk about fear. That annoying little voice in your head that pops up whenever you're about to do something new. You know, the one that whispers stuff like:

"What if you fail?"

"What if people laugh at you?"

"What if this is the worst mistake of your life?"

I remember the first time I had to speak in front of my class. It was just a two-minute presentation, but to me, it felt like I was about to deliver a TED Talk in front of the entire world.

As I walked to the front, my heart was racing, my palms were sweaty (mom's spaghetti, anyone?), and my brain was already planning my escape route.

And then, in the middle of my speech, I messed up. I forgot a word, stumbled, and—gasp—paused for what felt like five hours.

But guess what? Nobody cared. The world didn't end. My classmates didn't throw tomatoes at me. In fact, some of them were probably too busy daydreaming about lunch to even notice my mistake.

That's when I realized: Fear is a drama queen. It makes everything seem 100 times worse than it actually is.

Fear Loves Exaggeration (And It's Lying to You)

Fear isn't all bad. It's meant to protect us from actual danger, like running into a wild bear (which, unless your school is in the jungle, probably isn't happening).

But most of the time, fear overreacts.

Fear says: "If you try and fail, everyone will remember it forever."

Reality: People forget things faster than you think. (Can you even remember what your friend wore yesterday?)

Fear says: "If you step out of your comfort zone, you'll embarrass yourself."

Reality: Even if you do, people respect effort more than perfection.

Fear says: "You're not ready yet."

Reality: Nobody ever feels ready. You just start, and the confidence comes later.

Aha Moment: Fear is Just a Speed Bump, Not a Dead End

Fear will always be there, but you get to decide if it stops you. Successful people don't have less fear—they just don't let it control them.

Think about it: Every actor, singer, athlete, or entrepreneur has felt fear before a big moment. The difference? They do it anyway.

How to Handle Fear Like a Boss

✓ Step 1: Call It Out – When fear starts whispering worst-case scenarios, ask yourself: "Is this actually true, or is my brain being dramatic?"

✓ Step 2: Do It Scared – Waiting until you're "not afraid" is a trap. Confidence comes from doing things, not from thinking about doing them.

✓ Step 3: Collect Your Wins – Start small. Speak up in class once. Try a new hobby. Take note of every time you face fear and survive—it builds proof that you're braver than you think.

✓ Step 4: Laugh at Fear – Seriously. Fear hates being laughed at. Next time it tells you "You can't do this," respond with "Watch me."

Final Thoughts (AKA Why You Need to Ignore Fear's Drama)

Fear isn't the enemy—letting it control you is. The more you challenge it, the weaker it gets.

So go ahead—sign up for that competition, raise your hand, take that risk. You don't need to wait to be fearless. You just need to act despite the fear.

Because the truth? The scariest things often lead to the best things.

And worst case? You get a funny story out of it.

CHAPTER FIVE

LIFE IS AWKWARD, AND THAT'S BEAUTIFUL

The Time I Waved at a Stranger (And Other Embarrassing Moments)

Let me tell you about the most awkward moment of my life. (Okay, one of them—there are too many to count.)

I was walking down the street when I saw a girl from my school waving at me. Naturally, I smiled and waved back, because I am a polite and friendly human being.

Except... she wasn't waving at me.

She was waving at her friend behind me.

So there I was, standing in the middle of the road, hand in the air like an idiot, wondering if disappearing into the ground was an option.

And that's when I realized: Life is just a series of awkward moments.

Saying "You too" when the waiter says "Enjoy your meal."

Trying to push a "pull" door in front of people.

Accidentally calling your teacher "mom."

Tripping over absolutely nothing.

And no matter how cool, confident, or put-together someone looks, trust me—they have their own embarrassing stories.

Awkwardness: The Great Equalizer

You ever notice how awkward moments stick in your mind for years, but when someone else does something embarrassing, you forget it in like five minutes?

That's because we overanalyze ourselves way more than anyone else does.

Nobody's walking around remembering that time you mispronounced a word or laughed too loudly. (And if they are, well... that's weird.)

Why Awkwardness is Actually Awesome

Instead of cringing at awkward moments, here's why you should embrace them:

✓ It Makes You Relatable – Nobody connects with "perfect" people. We like people who are real, goofy, and imperfect—because that's everyone.

✓ It's Proof You're Living – If you're never awkward, you're probably never trying new things. And that would be a tragedy.

✓ It Gives You the Best Stories – Think about it: The funniest stories in life are always the awkward ones.

How to Handle Awkwardness Like a Pro

✓ Step 1: Laugh It Off – If you trip, mess up, or say something weird—own it. Make a joke, smile, and move on. Confidence isn't never messing up; it's handling it well when you do.

✓ Step 2: Remember Nobody Cares That Much – People are too busy overthinking their awkward moments to focus on yours.

✓ Step 3: Flip the Perspective – Instead of thinking, "That was so embarrassing," think, "That was hilarious." Imagine telling the story to your friends later—it instantly becomes less cringeworthy.

✓ Step 4: Accept That Life is Just... Weird – The sooner you embrace awkwardness, the more fun life gets. Awkwardness means you're out there, experiencing things, and being human.

Final Thoughts (AKA Why You Should Celebrate the Awkward)

Life is awkward. You can either stress about it or laugh at it. (Spoiler: Laughing is more fun.)

So next time you trip in public, stutter during a speech, or say something completely random—just smile, shake it off, and move on.

Because the truth? Everyone else is just as awkward as you. They're just better at hiding it.

CHAPTER SIX

PROCRASTINATION IS A FRENEMY

The Time I Became a Pro at Doing Nothing

Let me introduce you to my long-time, on-and-off, toxic relationship: Procrastination.

It all started one fine day when I had a big assignment due. Instead of working on it like a responsible human being, I thought:

"I'll start in five minutes."

Five minutes turned into watching one YouTube video. Which turned into scrolling Instagram. Which turned into reorganizing my entire desk (because suddenly, that felt super important).

And before I knew it, it was 11:59 PM, and I was having a full-blown panic attack, typing like my life depended on it.

This cycle? It repeated many times.

Until one day, I realized something: Procrastination is not my friend. But it's also not my enemy. It's a frenemy.

Why We Procrastinate (And Why It Feels So Good in the Moment)

Procrastination seems harmless at first. I mean, who doesn't want an extra break? But it always comes back to bite us.

Here's what actually happens in our brains when we procrastinate:

✓ We want to avoid discomfort. (That assignment seems hard, so we distract ourselves.)

✓ We crave instant rewards. (Watching a funny video = immediate happiness.)

✓ We lie to ourselves. ("I work better under pressure"—Yeah, sure.)

And before we know it, we're stuck in the "Why am I like this?" spiral.

The Myth of "Last-Minute Genius"

A lot of us believe we work better under pressure. But let's be real—cramming at 2 AM isn't genius. It's stress.

If last-minute work actually made us more productive, we wouldn't end up:

Forgetting important details.

Rushing through things and making mistakes.

Promising ourselves, "I'll never do this again"... and then doing it again.

So yeah, procrastination feels good at first, but future-you? They're going to suffer.

How to Outsmart Procrastination (Without Hating Your Life)

✓ Step 1: The "Just 5 Minutes" Trick – Tell yourself, "I'll do this for just five minutes." Most of the time, starting is the hardest part—once you begin, you'll keep going.

✓ Step 2: Make It Fun (Or at Least Less Boring) – Hate studying? Turn it into a challenge, play music, or reward yourself after. If something feels fun, you'll avoid it less.

✓ Step 3: The 2-Minute Rule – If a task takes less than two minutes, do it immediately. No "later," no excuses. Small wins add up.

✓ Step 4: Romanticize Productivity – Buy fancy stationery, light a candle, act like you're in a movie montage. Sometimes, tricking your brain works.

✓ Step 5: Forgive Yourself, But Do Better – You're not lazy; you're human. If you procrastinate today, don't waste time feeling guilty—just make a plan and start fresh tomorrow.

Final Thoughts (AKA Why You Should Stop Lying to Yourself)

Procrastination feels good in the moment, but stress isn't worth it.

You don't need to be perfect. Just start. Even if it's messy, even if it's slow—your future self will thank you.

And hey, next time you catch yourself avoiding work, just remember: The faster you finish, the faster you get to relax for real.

CHAPTER SEVEN

The Myth of Having It All Together

Spoiler Alert: Nobody Knows What They're Doing

You know those people who seem to have their whole life figured out? Perfect grades, perfect outfits, perfect Instagram feeds?

Yeah. They're faking it.

I used to think everyone else had life together—except me. While I was busy forgetting assignments and tripping over my own feet, everyone else looked like they had a detailed 10-year plan.

But then, something amazing happened. I got to know some of those "perfect" people. And guess what? They were just as lost as I was.

They were just better at pretending.

And that's when I realized: Nobody has it all together. They're just winging it at different levels of confidence.

Why "Having It All Together" is a Scam

We grow up thinking that by a certain age, we'll magically become responsible, confident, and organized. But here's what actually happens:

✓ 9-year-old me: By 16, I'll be super mature and know everything

✓ 16-year-old me: Okay, maybe by 20.

✓ 20-year-old me: Let's aim for 25.

✓ 25-year-old me (probably): Lol.

Truth is, nobody wakes up one day and suddenly has life all figured out. Adults? They don't have a secret manual. They're just making educated guesses.

And those people who look like they're doing everything right? They still doubt themselves. They just don't show it.

The Instagram Illusion

Social media makes it worse. You only see the highlights of people's lives:

That person who always looks great? Took 200 photos before picking the perfect one.

That straight-A student? Probably crying over exams just like you.

That "effortlessly cool" person? Spends hours planning their outfits.

Nobody's life is as perfect as it looks online. You're comparing your behind-the-scenes to someone else's edited version.

So, What's the Secret?...There is no secret.

The people who look like they "have it all together" aren't perfect. They're just doing their best—and that's all you need to do, too.

How to Be Okay with Not Having It All Together

✓ Step 1: Accept the Chaos – Life isn't supposed to be perfectly organized. It's messy, unpredictable, and full of surprises. That's what makes it interesting.

✓ Step 2: Stop Comparing Your Chapter 1 to Someone Else's Chapter 20 – Everyone moves at their own pace. You're not behind; you're just on your own timeline.

✓ Step 3: Focus on Progress, Not Perfection – You don't need to have your entire future planned. Just take one step at a time.

✔ Step 4: Laugh at the Mess – Tripped in public? Lost your homework? Forgot what day it is? Welcome to being human. Make a joke and move on.

Final Thoughts (AKA You're Doing Fine, I Promise)

Nobody has all the answers. Not me, not your teachers, not even your super-organized friend who color-codes everything.

We're all figuring it out as we go. And that's okay.

So next time you feel like you're the only one who doesn't have life under control, just remember: Neither does anyone else. They're just better at pretending.

CHAPTER EIGHT

PEOPLE ARE WEIRD (AND SO ARE YOU)

Let's Talk About That One Kid Who Meows in Class

Every school has that one person. You know, the one who randomly meows in the middle of a lecture, collects keychains shaped like vegetables, or insists on eating only one color of food each day.

And if you're thinking, "Wait, my school doesn't have someone like that," then... congratulations! You might be that person.

Here's the truth: Everyone is weird.

Some people just hide it better than others.

Weird is the Default Setting

Ever notice how little kids don't care about being "normal"? They'll wear mismatched socks, have full conversations with stuffed animals, and proudly tell strangers about the worm they found on the ground.

But as we grow up, we start worrying about what people think. So, we hide the weird parts of ourselves to fit in.

Except... why?

Being weird isn't a bad thing. It's what makes life interesting. Imagine a world where everyone acted the same, dressed the same, and talked the same. Boring.

The Myth of "Normal"

Spoiler: There is no such thing as normal.

Think about it: What's considered normal in one place is totally weird somewhere else.

Eating with chopsticks? Normal in Japan, confusing for some people elsewhere.

Wearing socks with sandals? A crime in fashion, yet some dads proudly do it.

Talking to yourself? Apparently weird—until you call it "self-motivation."

So really, normal is just a social construct. And if it doesn't exist, why are we all trying so hard to be it?

Why Embracing Your Weirdness is a Superpower

Instead of hiding your weird side, try owning it. Here's why:

✔ Weird People are Memorable – The most interesting people in history were not normal. Einstein had wild hair and hated socks. Steve Jobs wore the same turtleneck every day. Being different makes you stand out.

✔ It's More Fun – Pretending to be someone you're not is exhausting. Being your true, weird self? Way more enjoyable.

✔ You'll Attract the Right People – The more you embrace your weirdness, the more you'll find people who actually like you for who you are. And those friendships? Way better than fake ones.

How to Be Confident in Your Weirdness

✔ Step 1: Accept That Everyone is Weird – Even the "cool" people have their quirks. They just hide them better.

✔ Step 2: Own It – Like making up weird dance moves? Do it. Obsessed with obscure facts about dinosaurs? Talk about it. The more comfortable you are with your quirks, the less people will judge.

✔ Step 3: Find Your Fellow Weirdos – Life is more fun when you surround yourself with people who appreciate your brand of weird. Find your tribe.

✓ Step 4: Laugh at Yourself – If you trip, say something awkward, or accidentally call your teacher "mom" (again)—just laugh. Confidence isn't about being flawless, it's about owning your flaws.

Final Thoughts (AKA Why You Should Stop Hiding Your Weird Side)

Weirdness isn't a flaw. It's what makes you you.

So stop trying to fit into a box that doesn't even exist. Be loud, be awkward, be a little strange—because the best people in life are the ones who don't care about being "normal."

And if anyone ever calls you weird? Just say, "Thank you."

CHAPTER NINE

STOP WAITING FOR THE "RIGHT TIME"

The Myth of Perfect Timing (And Why It's a Scam)

Let me guess—you've told yourself something like this before:

✔ "I'll start working out... but only after exams."

✔ "I'll finally learn to play the guitar... but I need the 'right mindset' first."

✔ "I'll follow my dreams... but right now isn't the perfect time."

Sound familiar? Yeah. Me too.

For the longest time, I waited for the perfect moment to do

things. I thought I needed the stars to align, the universe to send me a sign, and my life to be completely stress-free before I could start.

You know what happened?

Nothing.

Because here's the secret: The "right time" doesn't exist. It's just an excuse we use when we're scared to start.

Why We Keep Waiting (And Why It's a Trap)

We trick ourselves into thinking that future-us will be more motivated, more confident, or just better than present-us.

Except... future-us is just regular us, but slightly older.

If you can't start today, what makes you think you'll magically start tomorrow?

Waiting for the "right time" is just a fancy way of procrastinating. It's like telling yourself, "I'll jump in the pool once I feel ready," but never actually getting in because the water always feels cold at first.

Reality Check: Everyone Who Starts is Unprepared

Think of the most successful people you know. Did they wait until everything was perfect before they started? Nope.

Every athlete was once a beginner who sucked at their sport.

Every famous musician played terribly before they got good.

Every confident person was once nervous.

Nobody starts at 100%. You just start messy and figure it out along the way.

How to Stop Waiting and Just Start

✓ Step 1: Realize That "Later" is a Lie – If you won't start today, you probably won't start later. Future-you is not a different person.

✓ Step 2: Start Small (Like, Tiny-Small) – Want to work out? Do one push-up. Want to write a book? Start with one sentence. Action beats waiting.

✓ Step 3: Accept That It Won't Be Perfect – Perfection isn't required. Progress is. Just do something.

✓ Step 4: Set a Ridiculously Easy Goal – Instead of saying, "I'll study for five hours tomorrow," say, "I'll study for five minutes today." Once you start, you'll likely keep going.

✓ Step 5: Call Yourself Out – Next time you say, "I'll do it later," ask yourself, "Why not now?" If there's no good reason, start.

Final Thoughts (AKA Why You Should Stop Making Excuses)

The best time to start? Yesterday.

The second-best time? Right now.

Doing nothing guarantees failure. Doing something, even if it's small and messy, means you're already ahead of the people still waiting for the "right time."

So stop waiting. Stop overthinking. Just take one small step today.

Because the truth is... the only "right time" is the moment you decide to start.

CHAPTER TEN

LEARN TO LAUGH AT YOURSELF

Because Life is Basically One Big Embarrassing Moment

Let's be real—no matter how hard you try to be cool, life will find a way to embarrass you.

✓ You'll trip in public for absolutely no reason.

✓ You'll send a text meant for your friend to your teacher.

✓ You'll confidently answer a question in class... and be completely wrong.

The faster you learn to laugh at yourself, the easier life gets.

Because here's the truth: Nobody actually cares as much as you think.

The Day I Learned This the Hard Way

I once called my teacher Mom in front of the entire class.

It was a normal day, and I was half-asleep when she asked me a question. Without thinking, I responded with, "Yes, Mom?"

Silence.

Then the class erupted into laughter. I wanted the ground to open up and swallow me whole. But then, something unexpected happened—my teacher started laughing too.

And at that moment, I realized: If she could laugh, so could I.

So, I did. And just like that, the embarrassment faded.

Why Taking Yourself Too Seriously is Exhausting

Some people are terrified of looking foolish. They spend their whole lives trying to be perfect, never making mistakes, never being awkward, never slipping up.

Sounds exhausting, right?

The truth is, everyone has embarrassing moments. The difference between confident people and insecure people? Confident people own their awkwardness instead of hiding from it.

The Magic of Laughing at Yourself

✓ It Makes You Instantly More Confident – When you're not afraid of embarrassment, nothing can hold you back.

✓ People Like You More – Nobody likes someone who acts perfect all the time. But someone who can joke about their own mistakes? Instantly relatable.

✓ It Stops Embarrassment in Its Tracks – The moment you laugh at yourself, you take away people's power to tease you.

How to Start Laughing at Yourself

✓ Step 1: Catch Yourself Overreacting – The next time you feel embarrassed, ask: "Will this matter in a week? In a year?" (Hint: It won't.)

✓ Step 2: Pretend It's a Movie Scene – If this happened to a character in a movie, wouldn't it be funny? Imagine you're watching yourself from the outside.

✓ Step 3: Make the Joke First – If you mess up, be the first to laugh. It throws people off in the best way possible.

✓ Step 4: Remember, Everyone Has Their Moments – That person you think is laughing at you? They've probably done something just as embarrassing (if not worse).

Final Thoughts (AKA Why You Should Start Finding Yourself Funny)

At the end of the day, nobody remembers your awkward moments as much as you do. The world moves on fast.

So instead of cringing at your mistakes, laugh at them. Enjoy the chaos. Because life is too short to take yourself that seriously.

And trust me—one day, the thing you're embarrassed about today will be your funniest story.

CHAPTER ELEVEN

THE POWER OF SAYING "NO"

Because You're Not a Doormat (Unless You Want to Be One)

Ever agreed to something you didn't want to do just to avoid feeling guilty?

✓ "Sure, I'll help you with your project (even though I have zero free time)."

✓ "Yeah, I'll come to that event (even though I'd rather stay home in my pajamas)."

✓ "Okay, I'll let you copy my homework (even though I spent hours doing it myself)."

Sound familiar? If so, congrats—you might be a people-pleaser.

But here's the truth: Saying "yes" to everything is exhausting. And worse? It makes people take advantage of you.

Why We Struggle to Say No

Most of us have been raised to be polite, helpful, and nice. We don't want to disappoint people, make them mad, or seem rude.

So we keep saying "yes." Even when we don't want to. Even when it drains us.

But newsflash: You can be kind AND still say "no."

The Cost of Always Saying Yes

If you agree to everything, you're basically signing up for:

? Less time for yourself – Your energy isn't infinite. If you waste it on things you don't care about, you'll have none left for what actually matters.

? More stress – The more you pile on, the closer you get to burnout. And spoiler: burnout is NOT fun.

? People taking advantage of you – The more you say yes, the more people expect from you. Soon, you're the "go-to" person for everything—and not in a good way.

How to Master the Art of Saying No (Without Feeling Guilty)

✔ Step 1: Realize You Don't Owe Anyone an Explanation – "No" is a full sentence. You don't need a dramatic excuse.

✔ Step 2: Be Polite, But Firm – Try, "I appreciate it, but I can't." Or "I'm busy, but thanks for thinking of me."

✔ Step 3: Practice With Small Things – Start with tiny refusals, like saying no to an extra task or turning down an event you don't want to go to.

✔ Step 4: Stop Overthinking How People Will React – Most of the time, people accept a "no" and move on. And if they don't? That's their problem, not yours.

The Power of Protecting Your Time

Imagine if you only said "yes" to things you actually wanted to do.

More time for yourself.

Less stress.

Better relationships (with people who actually respect your boundaries).

Sounds pretty great, right?

Final Thoughts (AKA Why No is Your Superpower)

Saying "no" doesn't make you mean. It doesn't make you selfish. It makes you someone who respects their own time, energy, and well-being.

So next time you're about to agree to something you don't want to do, ask yourself: Do I actually want this? If not, say no. Politely. Firmly. Guilt-free.

Because your time is precious. And the more you protect it, the more you can focus on what truly matters.

CHAPTER TWELVE

CELEBRATE THE LITTLE THINGS

Because Life is Made of Tiny Wins (Not Just the Big Ones)

We've all been there: waiting for the big moment to celebrate. You know, that one grand event that'll make everything worth it.

✓ "I'll celebrate when I get the promotion."

✓ "I'll party when I graduate."

✓ "I'll treat myself when I finally lose those 10 pounds."

But here's the problem: Life is happening right now. And if you wait for the big moments to celebrate, you'll miss all the little wins in between.

Why You Need to Celebrate the Small Stuff

When was the last time you took a moment to appreciate something tiny but meaningful?

✓ Managed to get out of bed before noon on a Saturday? Celebrate it.

✓ Finished that homework assignment you've been avoiding for days? Celebrate it.

✓ Didn't hit snooze for once and actually made it to class on time? Celebrate it!

The truth is, the little victories matter just as much as the big ones. In fact, they're often the ones that add up to the big wins.

The Danger of Only Celebrating Big Milestones

If you only celebrate when you reach the "big goals," you're essentially telling yourself, "I'm not good enough until I achieve this one thing."

That's a terrible mindset. It's like only eating dessert when you've finished your entire meal. What about the bread? The sides?

If we don't acknowledge the small victories, we risk feeling like we're constantly falling short. But when we celebrate each little win, we build momentum and self-worth.

How to Start Celebrating the Little Things

✓ Step 1: Acknowledge Your Progress – Instead of dismissing small victories, take a moment to notice them. "Hey, I made progress today." That's worth celebrating.

✓ Step 2: Find Joy in Everyday Moments – Did you make it through the week without crying over schoolwork? High five. Did you successfully make a smoothie that wasn't a disaster? Celebrate it.

✓ Step 3: Treat Yourself (Guilt-Free) – After hitting a tiny goal, treat yourself. Whether it's a chocolate bar or a 30-minute Netflix break, it's a well-earned reward.

✓ Step 4: Share Your Wins – Don't be shy about celebrating. Tell a friend about your accomplishment, no matter how small. They'll cheer you on, and you'll feel more motivated.

The Ripple Effect of Small Wins

Each small victory you celebrate builds your confidence. And confidence, my friend, is the fuel that propels you toward the bigger goals.

Imagine celebrating every step of the way:

Starting your project is a win.

Making progress on it is another win.

Finally finishing is just the cherry on top.

You'll be amazed at how much easier everything feels when you start acknowledging your small wins.

Final Thoughts (AKA Why You Should Throw a Party for Yourself)

Celebrating the little things doesn't make you vain or self-absorbed—it makes you human. It reminds you that life isn't just about the big milestones; it's about enjoying the journey, one small win at a time.

So start celebrating! Whether it's a tiny achievement or just making it through the day, give yourself a pat on the back. Because, in the end, the little things are what make life worth living.

CHAPTER THIRTEEN

BE YOUR OWN BIGGEST CHEERLEADER

Because No One Else Will Do It for You (Seriously, They Won't)

You know those people who always have someone cheering them on? They post their achievements, and it's like a personal fan club follows them around, clapping and shouting, "You're amazing!"

Well, guess what? That's not the reality for most of us.

And even if it is, you can't rely on someone else to cheer you on every time you need a boost. Here's the thing: The most important cheerleader in your life is YOU.

Why You're Your Own Best Support System

If you wait around for people to validate your worth, you might be waiting forever. Sure, encouragement from friends and family is awesome, but it doesn't always show up when you need it.

That's why it's crucial to learn how to cheer yourself on—loudly.

Here's why:

✔ You know yourself best – You understand what drives you, what challenges you, and what makes you feel unstoppable. Only you can truly appreciate your journey.

✔ You control the narrative – When you cheer for yourself, you're telling the world that you're proud of your progress, no matter how small.

✔ Self-encouragement builds resilience – The more you cheer for yourself, the easier it gets to keep going even when things are tough.

The Day I Realized I Wasn't My Own Cheerleader

I remember the time when I finished a huge project at school. It was stressful, I lost sleep, and I nearly gave up halfway through. But when I handed it in and got a great grade, I didn't take a moment to celebrate. I didn't even pat myself on the back.

I just moved on to the next task.

Then it hit me: Why was I waiting for someone else to say "Good job" when I knew I worked hard?

From that day on, I promised to cheer for myself—loudly and unapologetically.

How to Start Cheering for Yourself

✓ Step 1: Acknowledge Your Wins – When you achieve something, no matter how small, say, "I did that!" (Even if you're alone in your room, pretend you have a crowd cheering you on.)

✓ Step 2: Talk to Yourself Like a Best Friend – Would you let your best friend be hard on themselves? Of course not! So why do it to yourself? Be kind, encouraging, and loving toward yourself.

✓ Step 3: Give Yourself Rewards – You're working hard, so treat yourself. Whether it's a mini-break, a snack, or a fun activity, you deserve it.

✓ Step 4: Say Your Achievements Out Loud – It might feel awkward at first, but saying things like, "I'm proud of myself" helps boost your confidence. Plus, it's a reminder to yourself that you're worthy of recognition.

Why Self-Cheering is Key to Success

Every time you cheer for yourself, you're reinforcing the idea that you are capable, you are enough, and you are worthy of success.

This positive self-talk is the secret weapon that helps you keep pushing forward, even on tough days. When you can encourage yourself, you don't need external validation. You create your own source of motivation.

Final Thoughts (AKA Why You Should Be Your #1 Fan)

Imagine this: You're walking through life with a personal cheerleader inside your head. No one's clapping louder than you, and no one's more excited about your progress.

That's how you get through tough times. That's how you stay motivated.

So start cheering for yourself, because you deserve it. You're the one who knows the blood, sweat, and tears you've put into everything you do. Own that. Celebrate that. And above all, be your own biggest cheerleader.

CHAPTER FOURTEEN

LIFE IS SHORT—MAKE IT SWEET

Because You Only Get One Shot at This, So Why Not Enjoy It?

We're all guilty of getting caught up in the hustle. Whether it's school, work, or just the constant juggling act of life, we often forget something important: Life is short.

Sure, we all have responsibilities, deadlines, and to-do lists that feel never-ending. But that doesn't mean we should let the stress of life completely overshadow the sweetness of it.

So let's pause for a second and think about this: When was the last time you truly enjoyed the moment? Not just as a break from work, but as a celebration of life itself?

Why Life Feels Like It's Moving at Lightning Speed

It's a universal experience: time flies when you're busy. The more you rush from one thing to the next, the more you blink and realize months have passed.

And before you know it, the years start to pile up.

But here's the twist: The pace of life isn't the problem. The problem is how we choose to spend it.

If you're only focused on crossing things off your list, you'll miss the moments that actually make life worth living. The little things—like a spontaneous dance-off in your room, laughing with friends for no reason, or that first sip of your favorite drink after a long day.

The Sweetness of Life is Found in the Moments

Don't wait for the big events to enjoy life. The small moments—those are where the magic happens.

A text from your best friend that makes you smile.

The feeling of sunshine on your face when you step outside after a rainy day.

That satisfying moment when you finish a good book or binge-watch your favorite show.

The pure joy of a spontaneous adventure with no plans in mind.

These moments are what make life sweet. They're like little sugar sprinkles on top of the cake of life.

How to Make Your Life Sweet Right Now

✓ Step 1: Slow Down – Instead of rushing through everything, take a moment to appreciate where you are. Breathe. Look around. Soak it in. Life isn't a race.

✓ Step 2: Find Joy in the Simple Things – Whether it's a good cup of coffee, a funny meme, or a walk in the park, appreciate the little pleasures that bring a smile to your face.

✓ Step 3: Treat Yourself – You're working hard, so don't forget to treat yourself every now and then. Indulge in that guilty pleasure. Watch that random YouTube video. Take that afternoon nap.

✓ Step 4: Don't Take Life Too Seriously – Laugh at the absurdity of life. Embrace the messiness. Life is full of imperfections, but those are often the most memorable and sweetest parts.

The Power of a Sweet Life

When you start making life sweet, you shift your focus from the mundane to the magical. You start to realize that life isn't just about checking off boxes—it's about enjoying the journey, embracing the ups and downs, and finding joy even when things don't go as planned.

Each sweet moment you create builds your resilience. It reminds you that you have the power to shape your experience. And that's when life starts to feel like a beautiful adventure rather than a never-ending series of tasks.

Final Thoughts (AKA How to Savor Every Single Moment)

You've heard it before: Life is short. But maybe it's not about how long life is. It's about how you choose to live it.

So make it sweet. Celebrate the little moments. Treat yourself. And don't forget to laugh along the way. Because when you take the time to savor life, it becomes so much more than just a checklist. It becomes an experience—a sweet, joyful ride that's worth every second.

CHAPTER FIFTEEN

CONFIDENCE IS 90% FAKING IT

Because If You Wait for Confidence to Find You, You'll Be Waiting Forever

You know those people who seem to walk into a room and instantly command attention? The ones who just know how to own their space and look like they've got everything together? Well, I have a secret for you: They're faking it.

Yep, you heard me right. Most of the time, confidence isn't something you find—it's something you build. And if you wait around for confidence to come to you naturally, spoiler alert: it might never show up.

But here's the good news: You can fake it 'til you make it.

Why "Faking It" Actually Works

You might be thinking, "What? But if I'm faking confidence, doesn't that make me a fraud?"

Well, think of it this way: You know how some actors can play a character so convincingly that you forget they're just pretending? That's how confidence works. At first, it might feel awkward or unnatural, but the more you "fake it," the more it starts to feel real.

Here's the thing: Your brain doesn't always know the difference between reality and acting. When you act confident—standing tall, speaking clearly, making eye contact—your brain starts to believe that you are confident. And over time, those actions become part of who you are.

How to Fake Confidence Like a Pro

✓ Step 1: Stand Tall – Seriously. No slouching. When you straighten up and carry yourself with good posture, you not only look more confident, you feel more confident. Your brain gets the message: "Hey, I'm in control."

✓ Step 2: Speak Clearly – Ever notice how people who sound confident usually have a steady, clear voice? It's not magic—it's practice. Slow down, breathe, and say what you mean without rushing.

✓ Step 3: Fake Your Smile – Want to look confident? Smile. Even if you're not in the mood. Smiling releases endorphins and tricks your brain into feeling happier and more at ease. Plus, it makes you seem approachable and, let's be real, a lot more confident.

✓ Step 4: Make Eye Contact – Eye contact might feel awkward at first, especially when you're nervous, but it's a game-changer. It shows that you're engaged and confident in what you're saying.

✓ Step 5: Practice, Practice, Practice – Confidence isn't something that magically appears out of thin air. It's a skill, and like any skill, it gets better with practice. So practice speaking confidently, holding your posture, and walking with a sense of purpose. Eventually, it becomes second nature.

The Magic of Fake Confidence

It's not about pretending to be something you're not—it's about pretending until you actually start to believe it.

In the beginning, you might feel like you're acting. But eventually, your "fake" confidence will become real. It's like how a character in a play gradually becomes more comfortable in their role. The more you practice confidence, the more natural it becomes, and the more real it feels.

And here's the cool part: Once you start faking confidence, you'll be amazed at how much more you actually start to believe in yourself. It's like building a muscle—each time you flex that confidence muscle, it gets stronger.

Why You Don't Need to Be Perfect

Here's the real kicker: No one is 100% confident all the time. Everyone has moments of doubt. Even the people who seem like they have it all figured out. The key is learning how to fake it through those moments of uncertainty.

You're allowed to feel nervous, uncertain, or unsure. But don't let those feelings stop you from acting confident. Just because you feel nervous doesn't mean you can't look and act confident. The trick is to keep going, even when you're feeling anything but confident.

Final Thoughts (AKA Why Faking It Isn't Such a Bad Thing)

At the end of the day, confidence is a choice. It's something you can build, practice, and eventually own. So if you have to fake it until you make it, go ahead and do it.

The more you practice acting confident, the more you'll believe in yourself, and the more others will believe in you too. And soon enough, that "fake" confidence will become your superpower.

CHAPTER SIXTEEN

PERFECTION IS OVERRATED

Because Perfection is a Myth, and Honestly, It's Really Boring

Let's talk about something we all secretly chase: perfection. We all want to be the best, look the best, do the best, and achieve the best. But here's a hard truth: Perfection doesn't exist.

You can try to get everything perfect, but you'll end up running in circles, chasing a finish line that doesn't even exist. It's like trying to catch a unicorn—seems magical, but it's never going to happen.

So, let's just say it: Perfection is overrated.

Why We Obsess Over Perfection

It's easy to get caught in the trap of perfectionism, especially when social media feeds us a constant stream of "perfect" lives. But here's the thing: You're only seeing the highlight reel. You're not seeing the bloopers, the fails, or the struggles that came before the "perfect" moments.

We compare our behind-the-scenes to everyone else's highlight reel, and that's where the trouble starts. We think we need to have everything figured out, have everything polished, and show up as flawless versions of ourselves.

But guess what? It's impossible to be perfect, and it's way more fun to be real.

The Freedom in Imperfection

Here's the deal: When you stop aiming for perfection, you give yourself the freedom to be human.

You're allowed to make mistakes.

You're allowed to mess up and try again.

You're allowed to laugh at your failures instead of letting them define you.

When you give up the need to be perfect, you give yourself the space to grow, learn, and—dare I say it—enjoy the journey.

Why Imperfection Makes You Relatable

You know what's much more inspiring than perfection? Real people.

The ones who mess up but get back up. The ones who try

and fail and keep going. The ones who embrace their quirks and flaws and use them to build something incredible.

Perfection is boring because it's predictable. It's the same, safe, and polished. But imperfection? That's where the fun is. That's where the growth is. And that's where the magic happens.

How to Embrace Imperfection Like a Pro

✓ Step 1: Let Go of the "Shoulds" – Stop thinking you should be perfect. Stop comparing yourself to an unrealistic ideal. Just be yourself, flaws and all.

✓ Step 2: Fail Forward – Failure isn't the end. It's just part of the process. Every mistake is an opportunity to learn and grow. So, fail with pride, knowing you're one step closer to your next success.

✓ Step 3: Focus on Progress, Not Perfection – Instead of stressing over every little detail, focus on how far you've come. Celebrate progress, no matter how small.

✓ Step 4: Laugh at the Mess – When things don't go as planned, laugh it off. Life's messy, and that's what makes it interesting. Embrace the chaos and keep moving forward.

The Beauty of Imperfection

What makes life beautiful is its unpredictability. The little mistakes, the unexpected surprises, and the moments that aren't "perfect" but are real—that's where the beauty lies.

So, let go of the need to be flawless and start celebrating the messy, imperfect version of yourself. That's the version that makes life colorful, interesting, and worth living.

Final Thoughts (AKA Why You Should Stop Chasing Perfection)

Perfection is a lie. It's something we think we need to achieve, but when we actually get there, it's boring and unfulfilling. The real magic happens when you embrace your imperfections, flaws, and mistakes.

Stop wasting time trying to be perfect, and start enjoying the process of being yourself. Because at the end of the day, it's the imperfect moments that make life worth living.

CHAPTER SEVENTEEN

THE "WHAT WILL PEOPLE THINK?" TRAP

Because Their Opinions Are None of Your Business

Ever catch yourself hesitating before doing something because you're worried about what other people will think? Whether it's posting something online, speaking up in class, or just trying something new, we've all been there. The fear of judgment—of wondering what will people think?—holds us back more than we realize.

But here's a hard truth: Their opinions are none of your business.

Let's repeat that again: Their opinions are none of your business.

Why We Care About What Others Think

As humans, we're wired to care about what other people think. It's part of our social nature. We want to fit in, to be accepted, to belong. So it makes sense that we would feel nervous when we think others might judge us.

But here's the kicker: The opinions of others don't define your worth.

You don't need their approval to do what you want to do. And yet, we often let that fear control our decisions. We hold back from taking risks or going after our dreams because we're terrified of what people might say.

The Trap of Trying to Please Everyone

The problem with constantly worrying about what others think is that it turns into a never-ending cycle. You end up trying to please everyone—your friends, your family, your peers, and even strangers on the internet. And guess what? You can't please everyone.

Someone, somewhere, will always have something to say about what you're doing. And if you base your actions on their opinions, you'll constantly be chasing approval—and that's a trap.

Here's the real kicker: The more you try to fit into someone else's idea of who you should be, the more you lose yourself.

Why You Should Stop Caring About Their Opinions

Think about this: In 5 years, will it really matter what

someone thinks about that awkward thing you said in class or that picture you posted on social media? Nope.

The only opinions that matter are the ones that come from people who genuinely care about you. And those people? They're not judging you. They're supporting you, cheering you on, and encouraging you to be your best self.

The rest? They're just passing thoughts—like clouds floating by in the sky. They don't define who you are or where you're going.

How to Break Free From the "What Will People Think?" Trap

✓ Step 1: Remember Who You're Doing It For – Whether it's your dreams, your goals, or your happiness, remember that your actions are for you. Not for anyone else.

✓ Step 2: Embrace Imperfection – We're all imperfect. We all mess up. But that's okay! If people judge you for being human, that's on them, not you.

✓ Step 3: Focus on What You Can Control – You can't control what other people think, but you can control your own actions. So focus on what you can do and leave the rest

✓ Step 4: Ask Yourself: "Does This Matter in the Long Run?" – Will this moment of judgment matter in a month? A year? Five years? Probably not. So why let it stop you now?

The Freedom of Letting Go

When you stop worrying about what others think, you free yourself from unnecessary stress. You stop living in the shadow of other people's expectations, and you start living for yourself.

You become bold. You take risks. You chase your dreams. And you realize something important: The only person you need approval from is yourself.

Final Thoughts (AKA Why Their Opinions Don't Matter)

It's natural to care about what others think, but don't let that fear control your life. Their opinions don't define you, and they certainly don't dictate your worth.

So, the next time you catch yourself wondering, "What will people think?" ask yourself this instead: "Does it matter?"

Chances are, the answer is no. So go ahead—do it for yourself, not for them.

CHAPTER EIGHTEEN

LEARN TO PIVOT

Because Life Isn't Always Going to Go as Planned

We all have a plan, don't we? We map out our goals, set our intentions, and think we know exactly how things are going to unfold. But then—plot twist—life throws a curveball. Suddenly, the straight path you were on is no longer so straight.

This, my friend, is where the magic of learning to pivot comes in.

The Importance of Being Flexible

We love control. We love knowing what's coming next and having everything fall into place just as we imagined. But here's the reality: life doesn't work like that. Plans get messed up. Goals shift. Opportunities change. And guess what? That's perfectly okay.

When things don't go according to plan, you can either let it throw you off course, or you can pivot.

Pivoting isn't about giving up on your goals. It's about being adaptable and finding a new way to get to where you want to go, even if it's not the path you originally envisioned.

Why It's Hard to Pivot

At first, it's hard. We get attached to our plans. When things go wrong, we feel like we've failed. But here's the thing: you haven't failed. You've just encountered a detour.

You know what's harder than pivoting? Sticking to a plan that's no longer working. It's like trying to run a marathon on a road that's under construction—no matter how hard you try, you're not going to get very far.

Pivoting is your shortcut. It's the road less traveled that still gets you to your destination.

Examples of Pivoting in Real Life

You've probably heard stories of successful people who changed their direction midway and still ended up winning. Some of the greatest successes in history are stories of pivoting:

Steve Jobs didn't just build Apple by sticking to one thing. He pivoted through countless ideas, failures, and innovations to create the company we know today.

J.K. Rowling was rejected by publishers numerous times before Harry Potter became the global phenomenon it is. Had she quit, we would never have experienced the magic.

You! Yep, even you can pivot. Maybe you wanted to pursue a certain career, but a twist of fate led you in another direction. And guess what? You can still find success, even if it looks a little different from what you originally planned.

How to Pivot Like a Pro

✓ Step 1: Acknowledge the Change – Denial won't help. When things change, recognize it, accept it, and prepare to adjust.

✓ Step 2: Be Open to New Possibilities – The universe often throws curveballs for a reason. A change in plans could open the door to something even better than you originally imagined.

✓ Step 3: Trust Your Instincts – Pivoting can be scary, but if you trust your gut and follow the path that feels right for you, you'll find your way.

✓ Step 4: Take Action – It's easy to get stuck in the "what ifs" and never take that first step. But action leads to progress. Even a small pivot is better than standing still.

✓ Step 5: Embrace the Journey – The beauty of pivoting is that it's a journey in itself. You'll learn new things, grow in ways you never expected, and find new opportunities along the way.

The Benefits of Pivoting

Pivoting isn't just about changing your direction—it's about growth. The more you practice pivoting, the more flexible and resilient you become.

You'll:

Develop problem-solving skills.

Become more adaptable in uncertain situations.

Open yourself up to new opportunities you might have missed otherwise.

Final Thoughts (AKA Why Pivoting Is the Key to Success)

Life will never go exactly according to plan. But that's not a setback—it's an opportunity. Pivoting allows you to grow, learn, and adapt. It's the key to turning obstacles into stepping stones and challenges into opportunities.

So, the next time things don't go as expected, don't panic. Take a deep breath, adjust your approach, and pivot your way to success.

CHAPTER NINETEEN

YOUR INNER CRITIC IS A LIAR

Because That Voice in Your Head Isn't Telling the Whole Truth

You know that voice inside your head that tells you you're not good enough? That you'll never succeed? That you should give up now before you fail spectacularly? Yep, that's your inner critic.

And guess what? It's a liar.

Why Your Inner Critic Loves to Talk

Your inner critic isn't some mystical force—it's your brain doing what it thinks is best for you. It's trying to protect you from failure, disappointment, and embarrassment. But here's the thing: It's working overtime, creating problems that don't exist.

Why? Because your brain is naturally drawn to negativity. It's programmed to spot potential threats. Unfortunately, this can also mean it highlights every little mistake you make and blows it way out of proportion. And that's where your inner critic comes in, making everything seem worse than it actually is.

It's like that annoying friend who always tells you about every little flaw you have, even though you know they're exaggerating. Your inner critic is basically that friend who's on a constant mission to find problems that aren't even there.

The Problem with Listening to Your Inner Critic

When you listen to your inner critic, you start doubting yourself. You start believing that voice, thinking that you'll never be good enough or that you're bound to fail. And guess what? That's the exact thing that holds you back.

The more you believe in your inner critic, the more you let it dictate your actions, and the more it makes you play small. It convinces you to avoid risks, not chase your dreams, and stay in your comfort zone. It's like having a constant, nagging voice that says, "You can't do this," but the only problem is, it's wrong.

How to Silence Your Inner Critic

✓ Step 1: Recognize It's There – The first step in silencing your inner critic is realizing when it's speaking up. Start paying attention to the negative thoughts that pop into your mind, especially when you're about to try something new or challenging.

✓ Step 2: Challenge Its Lies – When your inner critic says, "You'll fail at this," ask yourself, "What evidence do I have that's true?" Spoiler alert: You'll probably find that your inner critic has no real evidence to back up its claims. It's just guessing.

✓ Step 3: Talk Back – You have the power to talk back to that voice. When it says, "You're not good enough," respond with, "Actually, I am. I've gotten through challenges before, and I can handle this one too." Own your strengths, remind yourself of past victories, and stop letting that voice control your narrative.

✓ Step 4: Don't Take It Personally – Your inner critic isn't you. It's just a voice. Don't take everything it says as gospel. It's like a bad roommate who makes a lot of noise but doesn't actually get to decide how you live.

✓ Step 5: Replace the Negative with Positive – The best way to silence your inner critic is to drown it out with positive affirmations. Replace "I can't" with "I can" and "I'm not good enough" with "I am enough."

The Power of Self-Compassion

Instead of listening to the negative voice in your head, try being compassionate toward yourself. We're all human. We make mistakes. We mess up. But that doesn't mean we're failures. It just means we're learning.

Treat yourself the way you would treat a friend. If a friend came to you with a mistake or a challenge, you wouldn't tell them they're a failure, would you? You'd offer them kindness and encouragement. You deserve that same treatment from yourself.

Why Self-Doubt Isn't the Same as Self-Defeat

Here's a secret: Everyone experiences self-doubt. It's not a sign that you're incapable or that you should give up. It's simply a sign that you're growing, challenging yourself, and stepping outside your comfort zone.

Self-doubt is normal. Self-defeat is optional.

Just because you feel doubt doesn't mean you're not capable. It just means you're pushing yourself to try new things, and that's when the magic happens.

Final Thoughts (AKA Why Your Inner Critic Needs to Sit Down and Shut Up)

Your inner critic is a liar, plain and simple. It's an exaggerator, a drama queen, and a perfectionist who doesn't know the full story. So, the next time that voice starts telling you you're not good enough, remind yourself that it's wrong.

You are enough. You are capable. You are worthy of success, and you have everything you need to get there. Don't let your inner critic steal your dreams. Silence it with confidence, self-compassion, and a healthy dose of "I got this."

CHAPTER TWENTY

GRATITUDE IS YOUR SECRET WEAPON

Because Appreciating What You Have Changes Everything

Imagine this: You wake up, and instead of dreading the day ahead, you think, Wow, I have another day to learn, grow, and eat snacks. Suddenly, your entire mood shifts. That's the power of gratitude. It's not some cheesy "just be happy" advice—it's a legit game-changer.

Gratitude is like a cheat code for life. It won't magically solve all your problems, but it will make you realize that even in the middle of chaos, there's always something good to hold onto.

Why We Forget to Be Grateful

Let's be real—our brains are wired to focus on what's wrong. It's easy to notice what we don't have, what's going badly, and what could be better. This is why people with everything—money, fame, success—can still feel miserable. They're stuck in a loop of "What's next?" instead of "What's already great?"

But here's the truth: No matter where you are in life, there's something to be grateful for.

You're breathing? Great start.

You have a bed? That's already better than millions of people.

You have Wi-Fi to read this? Life is truly a blessing.

When you start appreciating the small things, your perspective shifts. You stop feeling like life is one big struggle and start realizing that you actually have more than you think.

The Benefits of Gratitude (aka Why You Should Care)

Practicing gratitude isn't just about feeling good—it literally changes your brain. Studies have shown that gratitude:

✓ Reduces stress and anxiety – When you focus on what's good, you worry less about what's bad.

✓ Improves relationships – People love being around grateful humans. Nobody enjoys a chronic complainer.

✔ Boosts self-esteem – Instead of comparing yourself to others, you appreciate your own journey.

✔ Makes you happier – Shocking, right? Gratitude actually rewires your brain to focus more on joy.

How to Make Gratitude a Habit

Alright, so we know gratitude is powerful. But how do we actually use it daily?

1. Keep a Gratitude List

Every day, write down three things you're grateful for. They don't have to be deep or profound. It can be something as simple as:

My friend sent me a funny meme today.

My tea was the perfect temperature this morning.

I didn't trip while walking up the stairs (progress!).

The goal is to train your brain to notice the good instead of obsessing over the bad.

2. Say "Thank You" More Often

Gratitude isn't just about feeling thankful—it's about expressing it. Tell people you appreciate them. Thank your parents, your teachers, your friends. Even thank your alarm clock for waking you up (okay, maybe not).

The more you acknowledge what others do for you, the stronger your relationships become.

3. Reframe Your Problems

Instead of saying, "Ugh, I have so much homework," try "I'm lucky to have an education."

Instead of thinking, "I have to wake up early," remind yourself, "I have another day to make progress."

Sounds simple, but it works.

The Magic of Gratitude in Hard Times

"But what if my life is actually a mess?" you ask. That's when gratitude is most important.

Gratitude isn't about ignoring problems—it's about shifting your focus. Even on bad days, there's something to be thankful for. Maybe it's a small act of kindness. Maybe it's just the fact that you're surviving. But there's always something.

Final Thoughts (AKA Why Gratitude Wins Every Time)

Gratitude won't make your problems disappear, but it will make them feel smaller. When you start focusing on what's good, life becomes a lot brighter—even in the middle of challenges. So, start today. Look around. Find one thing to be grateful for. And watch how your entire perspective shifts.

CHAPTER TWENTY-ONE

BURNOUT IS REAL—REST ANYWAY

Because You Can't Pour from an Empty Cup (Or a Dead Battery)

Let's play a game. Imagine you're a phone. You start your day at 100%, feeling fresh and full of energy. But as the day goes on—school, homework, life drama, overthinking at 2 AM—your battery drains. You hit 5%, but instead of plugging yourself into a charger (a.k.a. RESTING), you're like, "Nah, I'll just keep going."

Fast forward a bit, and BOOM—your brain crashes. Congratulations, you've officially reached burnout.

Now, in a world that worships "the grind" and treats sleep like an optional hobby, burnout is almost seen as a badge of honor. Like, "Wow, you haven't slept in two days and finished an entire project while crying? That's impressive!"

No, it's NOT. It's terrifying.

So, let's settle this once and for all: burnout is NOT a sign of hard work—it's a sign that you need a nap, a snack, and some serious self-care.

Why We Burn Ourselves Out

We don't wake up one day and say, "You know what? I'd love to feel completely exhausted today." Nope. Burnout sneaks up on us like that one annoying relative at family gatherings—unexpected, exhausting, and very, very unwanted.

Here's how it usually happens:

1. You take on too much.

"I can totally do this," you say, adding five more things to your already full plate.

2. You ignore exhaustion.

You feel tired but think, "Let me just push through a little more." (Spoiler alert: It's never just a little more.)

3. Your brain turns into mashed potatoes.

Simple tasks start feeling impossible. Even deciding what to eat becomes a life crisis.

4. You officially crash.

No motivation. No energy. Just you, lying on your bed, questioning your life choices.

If this sounds even remotely familiar, congratulations—you're human! And humans need breaks.

How to Avoid Burnout Without Feeling Guilty

If you're someone who thinks resting is "wasting time," first of all, who hurt you? Second, here's how to rest without guilt:

✓ Step 1: Accept That You're Not a Robot

Even robots need recharging. Your brain and body do, too. So unless you're secretly an AI in disguise (in which case, wow, congrats), you need rest.

✓ Step 2: Schedule Breaks Like They're Important (Because They Are). Put "REST" on your to-do list. Make it official. Even if it's just 15 minutes to stare at the ceiling dramatically, your brain will thank you.

✓ Step 3: Do Something That Actually Relaxes You

Scrolling through social media? Not rest. Watching cat videos? Maybe. Taking a nap, reading, listening to music? Yes, yes, YES.

✓ Step 4: Say No (Without Apologizing)

If you're drowning in work, it's okay to say, "Sorry, I can't right now." Actually, scratch that—don't even say sorry. Just, "No, I need a break." Period. End of discussion.

✓ Step 5: Stop Glorifying Exhaustion

Bragging about how little you've slept or how overworked you are isn't cool. What's actually impressive? Having a healthy balance between working hard and resting smart.

The Science Behind Resting (Because Facts Matter)

If you still feel guilty about resting, let me hit you with some cold, hard science:

Your brain literally rewires itself while you rest. It organizes memories, processes information, and helps you solve problems better.

Rest makes you more productive. Taking breaks boosts focus, creativity, and energy. Basically, working non-stop = bad; resting smart = genius.

Burnout destroys motivation. The longer you ignore exhaustion, the harder it becomes to bounce back.

The Magic of Doing Absolutely Nothing

Have you ever just... sat there? No phone, no distractions, just you and your thoughts? It feels weird at first, but hear me out—it's amazing.

Your brain needs space to breathe. Some of the best ideas come when you're just chilling. That's why people get random "AHA!" moments in the shower or while lying in bed at night. Your brain loves those quiet moments.

So go ahead, do nothing for a bit. I promise, the world won't end.

Final Thoughts (AKA Why Rest is a Power Move, Not a Weakness)

Let's get real—if you keep running on empty, you're not being productive, you're self-destructing. And nobody wants that.

Think of yourself as a phone:

A dead phone is useless. So is a burnt-out brain.

Charging is non-negotiable. Just like resting.

You wouldn't ignore your phone's low battery warning. So don't ignore your own signs of exhaustion.

At the end of the day, your well-being is worth more than any task, deadline, or achievement. You are not a machine, a superhero, or a caffeine-fueled zombie (hopefully). You're a human. And humans deserve rest.

So, the next time someone tries to tell you that "sleep is for the weak," just smile and say, "So is running on empty." Then go take that nap.

CHAPTER TWENTY-TWO

SMALL WINS ARE BIG WINS

Because Progress is Still Progress (Even if It's Tiny)

Raise your hand if you've ever felt like you're not achieving enough. Now, keep your hand up if you've ignored small achievements because they "weren't a big deal." If your hand is still up, congratulations—you're part of the human species, where we love downplaying our own progress.

We live in a world that celebrates huge success stories. You hear about the teenager who became a billionaire, the athlete who broke world records, the artist who went viral overnight. What they don't tell you? Those massive wins are built on thousands of small wins.

Think of success like a puzzle. Each piece might look insignificant on its own, but put them all together, and BAM—you've got something incredible.

Why We Ignore Small Wins

Here's the problem: Our brains love instant gratification. We want to see big changes fast. So, when progress happens slowly, it feels like we're not getting anywhere.

You studied for an hour, but you're not a genius yet? "Ugh, what's the point?"

You exercised for a week but don't have six-pack abs? "Might as well give up."

You wrote a few pages of your book but didn't finish the whole thing? "Clearly, I'm not meant to be an author."

See the pattern? We judge progress too soon. But here's the truth: Every small step matters.

Why Small Wins Are Actually Huge

Think of anything great—learning an instrument, building confidence, writing a book, getting fit—it all starts small.

Every word you write = One step closer to finishing your book.

Every workout you do = A little bit stronger than yesterday.

Every time you speak up = A little more confidence.

It's not about overnight success. It's about consistent progress.

How to Celebrate Small Wins (Without Feeling Silly)

If you struggle to recognize your progress, it's time to change that. Here's how:

✓ Step 1: Track Your Wins (Yes, Even the Tiny Ones)

Write them down. All of them. "I woke up on time." "I didn't overthink for five minutes." "I finally cleaned my room."

It may seem small, but small wins add up. The more you track them, the more progress you'll see.

✓ Step 2: Stop Comparing Your Chapter 1 to Someone Else's Chapter 20

The only person you need to compare yourself to is past-you. Someone else's success is their journey. Yours is different, and that's okay.

✓ Step 3: Reward Yourself (Because You Deserve It)

Got through a tough day? Watch that episode. Eat that snack. Dance in your room. Rewards aren't just for finishing big tasks—they keep you motivated along the way.

✓ Step 4: Change Your Definition of Success

Instead of saying, "I'll be successful when I reach the top," try saying, "I'm successful because I'm moving forward." See the difference?

✔ Step 5: Keep Going (Even When It Feels Slow)

Success isn't about speed—it's about not stopping. Progress is still progress, even if it feels like you're moving at a snail's pace.

The Science Behind Small Wins (Yes, There's Science!)

Small wins trigger dopamine (the "feel-good" chemical) in your brain, making you more motivated to keep going.

Tiny progress builds momentum. The more small wins you stack up, the easier it is to stay consistent.

Your brain loves patterns. Once you start celebrating small wins, you train yourself to notice progress instead of focusing on failures.

Final Thoughts (AKA Why Small Wins Matter More Than You Think)

Imagine you're climbing a mountain. If you only focus on reaching the top, every step will feel frustratingly slow. But if you celebrate each step—the halfway point, the small breaks, the progress—you'll enjoy the journey.

So, the next time you feel like you're "not doing enough," take a step back and look at how far you've come.

Didn't quit? That's a win.

Tried your best? That's a win.

Took one tiny step forward? That's a huge win.

Success isn't about one big moment—it's about hundreds of small ones. Keep stacking up those wins. One day, you'll look back and realize—they were never small at all.

CHAPTER TWENTY-THREE

You're the Hero of Your Own Story

Because No One Else Can Live It for You

Imagine this: Your life is a movie. A big, epic, adventure-filled movie. Now, would you rather be the main character—the one who fights through struggles, learns, grows, and eventually wins—or be some random background character who just exists while life happens around them?

Exactly. You're the hero.

But here's the plot twist: Most people don't realize they're the hero of their own story. Instead, they wait. They wait for someone else to make things better, for the "right moment" to chase their dreams, or for some magical sign to tell them what to do. But heroes don't wait—they take charge.

Why We Forget We're the Hero

Let's be honest. It's easier to think "life just happens to me" than to accept that we're in control.

We blame circumstances. "I'd be successful if things were easier."

We compare too much. "Everyone else is ahead of me."

We doubt ourselves. "What if I mess up?"

But here's the truth: Every hero starts as an underdog.

Harry Potter? Started as an ordinary kid living under a staircase.

Spider-Man? Total nerd before getting bitten by a radioactive spider.

Your favorite successful person? Started from zero, just like you.

Every hero has a beginning. And this? This is yours.

The Hero's Journey (AKA Your Life in a Nutshell)

Ever noticed that every great story follows a similar pattern? It's called the Hero's Journey, and guess what? You're living it right now.

1. The Ordinary World – Everything feels normal. Maybe even boring.

2. The Call to Adventure – Something pushes you to change (a dream, a goal, a challenge).

3. The Doubt Phase – You wonder if you're good enough (spoiler: you are).

4. The Struggles – Every hero faces problems. Every. Single. One.

5. The Growth – You get stronger, smarter, and braver.

6. The Win – You achieve something you never thought you could.

7. The Next Adventure – Because the story never really ends.

Sound familiar? That's because you're in the middle of your own story right now.

How to Be the Hero of Your Own Life

If you're waiting for someone to come along and change your life... bad news: No one's coming.

But the good news? You don't need anyone to. You have everything you need to step up and own your story. Here's how:

✔ Step 1: Take Responsibility (Even When It's Hard)

Heroes don't blame life for their problems—they take charge. Instead of thinking, "Why is this happening to me?" ask, "How can I make this better?"

✓ Step 2: Get Comfortable with Failing

Every great hero messes up. But failing doesn't mean the story is over—it means you're in the middle of it.

Lost motivation? Try again.

Made a mistake? Learn from it.

Feel stuck? Keep moving.

Every failure is just part of the plot.

✓ Step 3: Start Before You Feel Ready

If you wait until you "feel ready," you'll wait forever. Start now. Even if you feel unprepared, even if you're scared. The best heroes take action before they feel brave.

✓ Step 4: Stop Comparing Your Journey to Others

Your story is yours. Stop measuring your success by what others are doing. The only person you need to compete with? Past-you.

✓ Step 5: Keep Going (Even When It's Hard)

Every hero hits a moment where they want to quit. But guess what? That's the part where they grow the most.

Final Thoughts (AKA Why This Is Your Story, No One Else's)

Imagine watching a movie where the main character just... gives up. No fight, no progress, just quits. Would you be inspired? Nope. Because we don't root for characters who sit back and let life happen to them.

And you? You're not here to be a background character. You're here to be the main character—the one who grows, learns, struggles, and eventually wins.

So, stop waiting. Stop thinking you're not good enough. Stop assuming your story doesn't matter. It does. You do.

And one day? When you look back, you'll see that every struggle, every small win, every moment of doubt was all part of a bigger story—yours. Now go, live it.

Motivational Takeaways

1. Motivational Takeaway
Failing doesn't make you a failure. It makes you human. And humans? We're designed to screw up, learn, and then screw up better next time.

2. Motivational Takeaway:
Step out of your comfort zone because growth only happens when you feel a little ridiculous. Or a lot. Either way, it's progress.

3. Motivational Takeaway:
Run your own race. Even if you're jogging in mismatched socks, at least you're moving forward.

4. Motivational Takeaway:
Fear only has power if you let it. Laugh in its face and keep going.

5. Motivational Takeaway:
Perfection is boring. Be awkward, be messy, be you.

6. Motivational Takeaway:
Procrastination isn't the enemy; it's just a distraction. Trick your brain by starting small—one step leads to momentum, and momentum leads to results.

7. Motivational Takeaway:
Stop striving for perfection. Focus on progress. Celebrate the small wins—like remembering to take the trash out on time.

8. Motivational Takeaway:
Embrace the weirdness—in yourself and others. Life's too short to be normal.

9. Motivational Takeaway:
Take the leap now. The only bad time to start is "never."

10. Motivational Takeaway:
Don't take yourself too seriously. Mistakes make great stories, and great stories make life worth living.

11.Motivational Takeaway:
Saying no isn't selfish—it's self-care. Protect your time and energy like it's your favorite snack.

12. Motivational Takeaway:
Happiness isn't in the grand gestures; it's in the tiny, everyday victories.

13. Motivational Takeaway:
Be kind to yourself. Celebrate your wins, big or small, and never stop believing in your potential.

14. Motivational Takeaway:
Don't wait for life to be perfect to enjoy it. Find the humor, embrace the mess, and live boldly.

15. Motivational Takeaway:
Fake it until you make it. Confidence isn't born—it's built, one awkward step at a time.

16. Motivational Takeaway:
Done is better than perfect. Life's too short to stress over the details no one notices.

17. Motivational Takeaway:
Live your life unapologetically. The right people will love you for who you are, mismatched shoes and all.

18. Motivational Takeaway:
When life doesn't go as planned, adapt. Some of the best moments happen when you embrace the unexpected.

19. Motivational Takeaway:
Be kinder to yourself. Silence the inner critic and replace it with a cheerleader.

20. Motivational Takeaway:
Gratitude turns what you have into enough. Focus on the good, and the bad won't feel so overwhelming.

21. Motivational Takeaway:
Rest is productive. Recharge, refocus, and come back stronger.

22. Motivational Takeaway:
Celebrate small wins. They're the building blocks of big success.

23. Motivational Takeaway:
Own your narrative. Be bold, take risks, and make your life a story worth telling.

Acknowledgment

Writing this book has been a wild ride—full of self-doubt, late-night overthinking, and moments where I seriously considered throwing my phone out the window. But somehow, I made it, and I have a lot of people (and a few life lessons) to thank for that.

First, thank you to everyone who supported me and also to those who didn't. Because let's be real—the ones who doubted me? You gave me even more motivation to prove you wrong. And for that, I'm truly grateful.

To my family—Papa (Udayshankar Vaishya), Maa (Shalini Vaishya), and everyone else—thank you for putting up with my "I'm writing, don't disturb me" moods, my sudden bursts of inspiration at weird hours, and my endless rambling about this book. Your love and patience deserve an award (or at least a long vacation—on me, someday).

To my sister, Manvi Gupta—thank you for your endless guidance, support, and for always being there to push me forward. Your words and wisdom have shaped not just this book, but me as a writer. The Unheard Soul is a masterpiece, and I'm lucky to have an author like you in my corner.

To my friends—you've been my biggest cheerleaders and my harshest critics, and honestly, I wouldn't have it any other way. Whether it was roasting my ideas, forcing me to take breaks, or reminding me why I started in the first place, you've been there through it all.

To every awkward, messy, and hilarious moment in my life—thank you for giving me something to write about. Without you, this book would be about as exciting as an instruction manual.

And finally, to you, the reader—thank you for picking up this book, for sticking with me through every chapter, and for embracing the chaos of life with me. If this book made you laugh, think, or feel even a little bit better about your own journey, then it was all worth it.

Now, go out there and be the hero of your own story. Because trust me, you're capable of more than you think.

About The Author

Garima Vaishya is a 15-year-old author from Ghatanji, a small town in Maharashtra, India. She started her writing journey during the COVID pandemic in 2020, and in 2024, she began working on her current book, marking a new chapter in her creative journey. While she has written before, it was mostly just for herself—her personal thoughts and reflections, never intended for the public eye... until now!

When she's not writing, Garima loves playing the flute and baking delicious treats. She's also a huge fan of reading and collecting books, with a special fondness for 101 Essays That Will Change the Way You Think and The Mountain Is You both by Brianna Wiest, which holds a special place on her shelf. Despite being from a small town, Garima has big dreams. She's passionate about cricket and is always on the lookout for new books to dive into.

Garima plans to write many more novels in the future, and her biggest dream is to become a New York Times best-selling author and win the Booker Prize. She knows that achieving this dream is possible only if her readers enjoy her work—so if you're reading this, you're a part of that journey!